The Notes from the Abyss

Suicidal Brain Memoires

by
Róża Lewanowicz

Table of Content

…What was the worst nightmare you had? Do you remember?

Mine was terrifying.
I was sitting in a room and realized someone else was before me. I looked up there, and I saw... myself. It was me, but not the me I knew. It was the person I had been scared of for most of my life—the core of me. First, I froze. Then, I wanted to say something to myself to calm down the person I saw. But she attacked me fiercely.

It took me at least five years to understand the dream's meaning. I had to go deep into myself. How did I do it?
I suffered.
I was tormented.
I was left alone by everyone.
I had depression.
I was hungry.
And every time I experienced any distress, I turned to God, reproaching, grieving, crying... But he wasn't keen to talk back. He was very quiet until His voice was silenced for good.

I understood.
The person I need to talk to is the woman from my nightmare because the stage of becoming independent wasn't closed. My mother rejected me as I am. I had to develop another personality, wear masks, be someone else to earn somebody's love. But love means acceptance for who I really am.

Now, I cannot expect this very acceptance from others. The only person who can do that is me.

***

My maternal grandmother killed herself fifteen years ago.
My mother killed herself five years ago.

I had been 'suicidal' for over thirty years, and both these deaths taught me one thing: I most probably will kill myself when the external circumstances are good. Not when I struggle the most with everyday obstacles, but when they're gone. I realized I have little time to fix what grandma and mother neglected and what led them straight into the abyss.

Death's Breath on My Neck

I call it "Black Hole", but it is more like a small, vicious bullet that repeatedly, yet every time, surprisingly, hits the human being right in the core of the soul. No matter what you do or decide, it always comes back, and the next attack is even more dreadful. It reminds me of the loop, but it's not so much determined by our choices and actions. The bullet just shows up, seems out of nowhere, hits and then starts to suck out whole the joy of life until... attacked person commits suicide.

I had been thinking for months about my late grandmother, who took her own life. I sometimes couldn't sleep or think about anything else, which was a desperate attempt to solve the ultimate problem: was it possible to save her? Who could help her? Was I able to do something?

First, I was angry with my family that they had ignored all the symptoms and hadn't been seeking psychiatric consultation. I wanted to see all of them behind bars for life... My mother did the most stupid thing she could: she threatened her mother - a very religious person - a hell for talking about suicide, unaware that, at that point, my grandma was in the state that made her unable to reason whatsoever, because the "Black Hole" was consuming her mind and body. She was unaware that she would follow the same path a decade later.

Today I know one thing: she wasn't able to not commit suicide. I have that certainty since my own "Black Hole" devours my mind and body.

If you tell the shrink that you don't want to live, you may be sent to the psychiatric ward. And there is nothing wrong with it as long as people who will treat you have the will to find out what, for real, causes your state. You need to look into your Black Hole and see it.

Since I was six, I constantly wanted to die. I think about death just as kids feel about ending the school year, as if it were a salvation. And even when I find some motivation to live further, my emotions are so damaged that the pain becomes unbearable... Inside, I am an old woman, for every day counts three times. Waking up is painful. Making decisions is painful. Ordinary activities hurt as hell...

Of course, the whole problem is not being loved by parents and carers. It concerns being forced to do things we don't want (when parents, not us, decide how our future should look). It may involve abuse, neglect, and all the evil stuff adult people do to little children... But many of us experienced these things, yet don't want to kill ourselves. So, the question is what kind of factor creates us, the kids with suicidal brains?

Answering is essential because it may help to understand why some people can handle the reality, though it's cruel, while others cannot bear even smaller weights.

It's loneliness. Being an outcast. This is the lack of bond that our mothers or somebody else should have built with us at this fundamental growth stage. And, I'm afraid, this loss is irreparable.

You can dig out of despair only by grabbing another person's hand and building a relationship. But what can we do when we are deprived of this fundamental skill and, what is worse, we are not aware of it?

Then we cannot build a relationship with ourselves.

Princess Diana and Princess Marilyn

If you were not loved by your parents and by nobody else whatsoever, but, unfortunately, you are pretty or sexy girl and, later on, a wise woman, you learn very quickly that your beauty and sex appeal may buy you a "love", which, is only some kind of attention and admiration.

Undoubtedly, neither Diana Spencer nor Marilyn Monroe had loving parents and carers as the little girls. They were not wanted, always rejected, and not good enough. Reading their biographies made my heart bleed in excruciating pain. But it took me some time to realise that both of them were 36 years old when they died tragically. And only when I turned 36 did I fully understand their situation.

This age is very special for women. The body changes rapidly. The face is no longer so shiny and fresh. It is hard to sustain a proper weight. And the mind, much brighter than before, starts to realise that the past is past, and the ageing cannot be stopped. Well, for a "normal" woman who has all stages of her psychological development closed, this is the time of new prospects. She may feel sad looking at the mirror and not seeing that smooth and lovely face, but she has many more reasons to live longer - family, children, friends, career, glass of wine in the evening, favourite TV series, etc. But, for us, the "sweet dolls", "little princesses", this is the end of everything, unless... we, by some miracle, become "aware" princesses.

In the case of Diana and Marilyn, the miracle didn't happen. The lines of their lives - filled with drug overuse, eating disorders, believing in superstitions and nonsense read from the tarot - had been leading straight to the doomed end.

Marilyn's real name was Norma. And if you glimpse the pictures taken while she was very young, you will see a normal-looking girl. Except she wasn't loved. She used her sharp mind (she was brilliant) to draw the attention of other people. "Boobs and butt" instead of intelligence and modesty. Platinum blonde hair and a pearl-white smile instead of a gentle look and a simple hairstyle.

The people "bought" it, yet the pain had been intensifying. Norma didn't feel the love the fans worldwide showed her...

Reading Diana's biography, written by Andrew Morton, was one of the least pleasant experiences of my life. Nobody cared about this girl. From the beginning, she was a huge disappointment, only because she wasn't a boy (interestingly, one of her sons was the same disappointment for not being a girl). When she married Charles, she was a child, and I am fully convinced she remained a child till her demise.

And she had been "selling" a fake picture of herself. Full of contradictions, she always knew how to make people's hearts beat faster. Innocent gaze under golden fringe, silent voice, proper pose, and, simultaneously, countless affairs (or gossip about them), controversial moves, interviews set up with the press she hated so much... supposedly. She hid behind charity work, which provided most people's admiration, so the pain seemed to fade. Her last days were filled with constant work, and her life was much too fast...

So about me... I am no longer pretty. The sweet doll disappeared. I am overweight and a little bit clumsy. My legs and arms look like fat sausages, and I'm constantly tired. I look like a normal woman, 40-something years old. Naturally, I felt an excruciating pain since I'd lost what I was buying people's admiration and attention for. Yet, I am alive. I have prospects. I've just received an offer of a good job, and my subsequent novels are to be printed. The pain didn't fade, but the awareness is keeping me vertical. And there is something much more critical - Faith.

I am not against charity work nor a career in show business, but I think that, in God's intention, our good is much more critical, for:

"What will anyone gain by winning the whole world and forfeiting his life? Or what can anyone offer in exchange for his life?" [Matthew, 16,26]

My grandmother killed herself. My whole family has denied the fact, and this is a huge family, which didn't change the fact that she committed suicide.

I write about it today because I know why she did it. I have always been far from judging her, and now, I am even less eager to condemn this act. I am angry because the leading cause has been given to me as some diabolic heritage, written down in my body, nervous system, and genes, and I feel as if I couldn't avoid it. I cannot rid myself of this pain and the defect within me.

What is interesting is that I was sure my mother would avoid that fate thanks to me, because I left her, I cut the contact, so she gained the motivation to live longer since she had someone else to blame for her misery. I was so wrong!

But I, like my grandmother, lost motivation and hope, and I see myself in a lost position. The only benefit of this situation is that I now know why my grandmother didn't want to live anymore.

This is an extraordinary moment - I found myself in a place where I see the core of myself. I am the true me, without masks and pretending. And this is awful and amazing at the same time. **Being me**, even if the truth is so appalling. I read the glitch in my source code, yet I don't think it's my fault. The glitch doesn't damage my source code completely - after all, the code's main feature is to be unbreakable unless... I want it to be destroyed. The decision is up to me. I am free, I can decide whether I am worth something or nothing. But the glitch says it doesn't depend on me, that I need another person to tell me whether I deserve to live. It compels me to constantly send a question, just as software programs do, to certain people, whether they would let me stay here, if I could do this or that, if I could be happy...

It is impossible to stop sending the questions just like that. The stage should have been closed a long time ago, I presume, when I was two years old, but since it didn't happen, I've been stuck in a loop, which means continuous searching for an object that could provide the correct answer. For my grandmother, it was her husband (replacing parents' figures), and, when he died, she lost the object, and everything her life had been built on collapsed, so she took her life one year later. I didn't take my own life, but I rejected the object... consciously, unaware that it would bring me to the edge of despair.

My existence was fake until then, though my feelings were always true. I didn't understand what they meant or their provenance. I was depressed, angry, and full of grief for a good reason. I didn't accept that because I couldn't find anyone who could give a good answer with a compassionate attitude. Well, not anyone but this particular person, so similar to my parents. And the only person like this, closest to me, is... me.

Meta-question

At some point, when we are grown-up or even very grown up people, who have own opinions and lots of experiences, we cannot simply ask the question small children send to their parents in different ways - usually, in non-verbal way. It in fact would mean behaving inappropriately, recklessly even. It is obvious, most of other people would not understand the background of such behaviour and we'd have more problems than before. Just look at inmates in prisons or addicted from drugs and alcohol.

No, when we are aware of our condition, the question is different of two reasons. First, it should be sent to the internal world of our minds not outside, to the wide (and mostly wild) world. Second, it must be verbalised. And, since this is a question regarding the question, we talk about meta-question:

"Is this particular question correct? Am I right asking it?"

I made that discovery when I realised that all the efforts of my parents and other carers had been focused on convincing me that my "demands" are wrong, e.g. the desire of meeting my own father, the need of spending time with my mother, so much concentrated on her own needs... So, I convinced myself that I am wrong. I stepped into the reality of auto-aggression, I stood against myself, against the divine design.

I am right though. I was always right, and the questions were appropriate all the time:

- am I worth of being loved? (since you, my parents, don't love me)

- am I worth of being alive? (since you, my mother, don't care about my basic needs)

- do I suffer for a good reason? (since everyone around me seem to find my situation as something good)

Yes, these were very good questions.

The Fatal Answer

Ok, let's sum up.

I've established that my questions sent to other people - parents, carers, teachers etc. - were correct.

I did receive the answers, and... every single time, it was negative, like:

"no, you don't deserve to live, unless..."

or:

"no, you cannot be unconditionally loved, unless..."

The trick is that we are created so that we won't rest in peace of heart and soul until the answer is correct, *ergo* positive, and this is an indisputable fact challenged by following generations.

If the answer is negative, as it was in my case, our bodies and minds send the question all the time by coercing us to make certain decisions that, not so rarely, harm us and the others. And the suicide is the final answer we give to ourselves.

I'll Die... Someday

I distinguish at least three main factors that may lead the person to the suicide.

First, negative answers to the questions, sent by the little child to the external world, the answers denying child's right to be loved and respected unconditionally, just as it is. A toddler, treated badly, cannot learn the respect for itself and the bad choices during its future life seem logic, since own parents did not behave properly.

Second, directly related to the first one, is that the kid will never have the chance to become an independent "human unit"; independent from the acceptance and love of the certain kind of people. Thus, as an adult person, he or she is constantly focused on searching for someone who will provide the prove that he or she can live and be happy. This lack of internal independence is crucial.

I had once a friend who had attempted to commit a suicide for three times after his wife left him. We couldn't understand this kind of attachment to any other person... Well, I did get the point after my grandma's demise and after my own "adventures" from the twilight zone. Sometimes, when we lose the object that have been this kind of approver for our existence and actions, we lose the base our lives were built on.

I have this feeling that I am not able to "catch" myself, that I am far away from my own core, which is not odd if I realise how much effort I put into searching for things that will prove I am worth of living. My mother's family respects only these members who work very hard... too hard, or persons who are ill. Once my grandmother couldn't work anymore, she escaped into countless diseases although the doctors had been convincing her she is fine. So, she had been bribing other doctors, most of them didn't even see her, and, couple years later, she had access to the pills that killed her...

And guess what? My own mother had been convincing me during my whole life that I am a lazy piece of s$*t, hence I was worthless, and her bad behaviour was totally justified. As a result, I am now killing myself by doing various things to demonstrate that I am not the lazy piece of s$*t instead of living my own life.

The third factor is a fear of the death. It sounds illogically but, in fact, this is very simple. We, people with "suicidal brains", are always deprived of control of our own lives and the suicide seems as the only thing in this world that may be in the reach of hand. The place, the time, the way... and no fear, no surprises. But, underneath these illusions, there is something much worse hidden: the story about how we almost died and how scared we were then. Our mother or other family member demanded the abortion; we had been beaten repeatedly as the very small babies; we had been left alone for many hours or with strange people, so we were afraid that our carer won't be back, and we will die without food and love... This is the worst lack of control we can imagine - not knowing when and how we will die, and that we... will die for sure. Someday.

My Dear Friend, Augustine

Sirach Book [7,36] says:

"In everything you do, remember your end, and you will never sin."

My favourite line in the Holy Bible so let me elaborate it.

We all die... someday soon. This is as much inevitable as unwelcome, but this thought, paradoxically, may let us live happy life (of course, if you believe in Almighty God who will open you the gates of the Paradise).

For many years, I had been focused on the words 'never sin'. I wanted to be innocent, pure, in order to not to be condemned and rejected. As you may easily assume, achieving this goal was impossible for me and caused lot of disappointment.

But over ten years ago, I changed the perspective by understanding that 'never sin', in fact, means 'always happy'. And I made the first "death bed test": I asked myself what I would regret the most if I'd know that I am going to die within next couple of months. I answered. And I did it. Later on, I had been making this test many times, until something broke...

Suddenly, I realised that I don't know what I want the most, what is so important that must be done immediately. I told the loved one that I love him (it didn't work but it helped me with other issues); I went to the paradise island for a vacation; I wrote a book (then more) etc.

There was this sad and unspoken thought in me: what's the point of all this, since I am going to die anyway?

The problem was death itself. The end. Absurdity of everything in the face of my own demise. I didn't know about the main problem I was writing about in previous posts, that I want to get this one certain "prize" I didn't receive long time ago and that I am not able to rationalise this issue any longer simply because I am older every year...

So, let's solve this equation since my whole life (and death) depends on it. I am absolutely aware of the one thing I was deprived of. I am also aware that, most likely, I won't get it. If I am not trying to get it - though I know it may be pointless - I lose the only motivation that keeps me alive. The result - impasse. Up this point, I was blocked by this outcome, until I remembered the last episode of House M.D. TV series: everybody dies. Something my late grandma did forget. We are not immortal, even the people our happiness seems to depend on.

Hence, the real result is: LOVE AND DO WHAT YOU WILL, there is no much time left.

In some way, people who are rich and famous are screwed. They have something that can be "traded" for "love". The same applies to very talented persons - they also may be helpful for others.

Imagine a young man, in the type of the Princes, who has many problems, whose parents didn't love him, but who was born in a wealthy family and the only future he can have is being even richer and famous... I bet he doesn't have to be handsome or too intelligent to gain the attention of certain women.

And the worst thing is that those people think it is good to have something to trade. Just look at these moronic mothers who convince their daughters that they must learn some skills (even if they are not capable in them), being all smiles no matter what, and demand nothing for themselves - and all these just for one thing: finding someone who will buy this fake picture, love and marry them... Pathetic.

So, people who have more fame and fortune than others may want to trade them, especially when everything else fails, e.g., things from the list below (you may replace "he" with "she").

He was trying to be nice.

He improved his behaviour, since everyone in his family was complaining.

He did all he could to please every person he met, even quitting the job he loved so much.

He engaged himself in charity work and launched a new, fantastic foundation.

He focused more on his look and wardrobe, started going to the gym, and changed his diet.

He quit smoking, limited drinking, and partying.

He became a supporter of many minority groups and movements.

He is trying to save the world.

He became Someone Else...

The trick is that Mr. Someone Else, not Him, married this beautiful woman.

Stigmatic

I wrote that I distinguish at least three factors that may lead a person to suicidal death, but there are two more I need to mention. These are two sides of the same coin: guilt and shame.

Mr./Ms. Someone else became who they are because of these two factors (though, of course, they don't have to kill themselves).

Since I can remember, I have been intimidated by my mother and, then, by other people. Now, I know that men and women who act like that feel ashamed and guilty for most of their lives. They simply need a convenient scapegoat to transfer their discomfort to, and there is no better one than a child. As a result, your life turns into a crime TV series, and you are always a suspect whose words and actions may be used against you.

People who haven't experienced this situation cannot understand how shame impacts existence. Even if there is no reason to be ashamed and even if we are no longer surrounded by persons who try to intimidate us, we find a way to feel bad anyway. And there is no more significant reason to be ashamed than that we are not loved (we were not loved when we needed it the most). We are "stigmatised" for life, and every second, we feel excruciating pain which we desperately try to avoid.

At this point, unfortunately, we too often make bad decisions, like running away or marrying the wrong person. All depends on the society we live in, e.g., in Poland, things I do and most of my achievements are seen as nothing as long as I don't get married and have children. I met my classmate once, and she called me a vagrant, a wanderer, although I have my own flat and an excellent job. She intimidated me, though I accomplished much more than she did (that was the point, probably).

Many successful people are unhappy because they constantly feel their own stigmas burning in their souls. There is always someone out there who doesn't love them, doesn't appreciate their efforts, and finds them worse or useless.

The guilt complements the tragedy. You are never pure enough, never worthy enough. You always have some debts to pay just because you were born, and you use the air. You so desperately want to be loved and accepted that you would do anything—even disappear.

PTSD

Did you ever wonder why some soldiers suffer from post-traumatic stress disorder and some do not, although both groups experienced the same traumatic events?

Well, since I was a soldier many years ago, and since I've suffered from PTSD, without being on a war, and since I heard countless stories about soldiers' mental problems, I will shed some light on this topic.

I had been experiencing trauma from the very beginning of my service, despite wearing the uniform being my dream, I think one of the biggest dreams in my life. I had encountered one particular problem I hadn't identified for a very long time: a lack of home. By 'home' I mean a place where I could feel safe and regenerate myself emotionally. I was the easiest target to abuse by predators (my supervisors), and during my weekend or holiday breaks, I had been abused by... my mother. I wasn't free from her yet and wasn't even fully aware that she was the reason for my various problems.

So, yes - I was a victim of physical and sexual abuse, and my own mother didn't care when I was telling her about it... And there was no place on Earth to escape.

There was an accident once when one of the recruits shot himself on his watch with his AK-47. This was something terrifying - a twenty-year-old boy lay down on the ground, put the barrel into his mouth, and pulled the trigger... The first and natural question was WHY? And you never guessed what the reason was. He was afraid of his parents because he had damaged his father's new car during the weekend break. Silly, right? Except it is not. He, like me, did not have the place to escape either. He was bullied and vulnerable.

People who are already traumatised by their families, especially by their own parents, have little chance of staying sane in environments like the army or situations like war, because they become even more traumatised within the following months and years. It is more likely they will have mental problems or even commit suicide.

Do I find this is the army's fault, after all? Yes! Because my commanders did break the law by abusing me just as commanders of the recruit who killed himself did not observe their duties properly by not watching over him. After his death, the main problem for them was whether stains of blood and brain on his uniform would be washable so that it could be reused... (And these are not even stories I heard from soldiers serving in Afghanistan.)

I am far from saying that people from dysfunctional families cannot serve their countries well. But it is very hard to find motivation for further effort when we also see the enemy on the 'friendly' side.

Real Reality

Do you like the TV series Elementary? I like it very much, but not because the crime mysteries, contemporary Sherlock Holmes, and a feminist version of Watson solve so smoothly in every single episode. I like the theme of Sherlock's addiction, how he copes with it, and how this struggle changes him within the following seasons.

First, the figure of the father is a vicious and relentless businessman who destroys everyone and everything, which may put his interests in jeopardy. Yet, when his son needed help, Morland Holmes did his job well: he sent the son to rehab, hired a sober companion, and determined obvious rules... I think that, subconsciously, the creators of the title solved another mystery concerning the reasons for people's addiction. Sherlock's father was a lousy parent, and, with drugs and reckless lifestyle, the son was calling for his attention, and... he received it. In this one moment, he wasn't left alone (with nannies, in boarding school); he got the help he needed as a grown-up man.

Second, the figure of the sponsor, whose fundamental instruction was not the twelve steps every therapy requires, but this one: if you want to stay sober, you must be egoistic. Of course, 'egoistic' is not the most adequate word, but the client should shift the meaning of certain expressions to understand how the objective reality works. Because an addicted person's reality is very unsettled, and he or she sees relationships in a completely different way than 'normal' people. If an old companion of binge drinking comes and wants to take the addict to rehab, the addict feels that, by refusing him or her, he is... egoistic, though it isn't true whatsoever.

And the third reason I like this TV series is that Sherlock did not become addicted to his father (or another person), because this is the basis of every addiction: being dependent on somebody else. Alcoholism or drug addiction only prolongs the relationship we had with our parents, a horrible relationship.

This is my struggle—being egoistic and refusing to do and think my mother's and her family's way. And I feel I am egoistic; hence, I feel bad. I feel very bad.

Shame, Shame, Shame

When I was writing about shame as one of the possible factors that may lead to suicidal thoughts, I meant being ashamed by the fact that... I love someone.

My vicious mother did not tell my biological father about being pregnant by him. He learnt about my existence when I was three and he was shocked. He came and demanded to see me. She disagreed and treated him like trash. But the more significant 'issue' for her was that I needed and missed him, and, at the age of three, I started asking where he is and why he doesn't visit us... Since she was brilliant, she found a way to cope with this inconvenient situation - she convinced me that missing and loving Daddy is inappropriate, rude, and... embarrassing.

Most of my relationships with men were based on this scheme, and I felt ashamed that I had feelings for them. And, what is not surprising, they all took advantage of my fragility.

The truth is, we have little to decide when it comes to what we feel. Emotions shouldn't be suppressed or denied, though they shouldn't be expressed in every situation either. So, if I am in love with someone, I need to be sure whether revealing these feelings would be good for me. But being ashamed of them is complete nonsense.

Case of Grace

I had a friend in the army - a young, bright, and beautiful woman, who was a lawyer before wearing the uniform. She had very... interesting relationships with the men. She could tell many stories about them, but the most interesting one I witnessed was her relationship with a guy she almost married. Her fiancé was so different than the rest of her lovers and 'beaus' I had pleasure or unpleasantness to meet with that I couldn't believe they are together... Old, ugly, stupid, and conservative misogynist, whose biggest problem was making career women. I asked my friend once, "Seriously? Him?!" But she was smitten and ready to serve him, iron his shirts, and spend the rest of her life with him. Her! The woman with higher education, CO in the army, platoon commander, war veteran, and, foremost, the woman who didn't want to have kids, never in her life!

Ok, I need to be honest - simultaneously, I was in a very similar relationship, which caused me to terminate the crying rivers of tears... And I was ready to let this man back to my life, but I bought my flat and, after couple of months of struggle in new reality, I realised I don't want to see this moron anymore, for I won't handle another liability. My friend from the army bought the flat too, I think six months later than me, and... she came to the same conclusion: "I have enough burdens to deal with, I don't want someone who will cause more trouble".

I encountered many women with similar experiences who kicked off bad partners after doing something brave or simply something independently, even when these guys were the fathers of their kids. That's why the Grace Kelly case has astonished me for years. This was a mystery. Her decision to marry this prince was... without any sense. I would understand it if she weren't such an independent, talented, and successful person. At first glance, she didn't need anyone. She could only be with a man who would adore her more and be her most considerable support in everything she was doing, so she had an even bigger chance to develop her talents. An old guy who locked her for life in the golden cage is the last option.

I have some new remarks regarding the 'case of Grace', because she wasn't the isolated incident in history. In fact, I may have something in common with her (which is why I am so obsessed with that sad story).

Of course, I am not as beautiful, and I didn't achieve amazing things like winning an Oscar, but I know too well how it feels to feel that things I do are not good enough, that I need to do something bigger, that I need to impress everyone, especially my rejective parents. Thus, instead of developing my talents, I am constantly unsatisfied with myself (because I am not the queen of the world yet).

Grace's story is not exactly the story of wasted talents, for she had been using her charm and countless virtues as a princess. However, this is a tale about an unhappy woman, and I, for example, don't want to be unhappy, so I use this biography as a warning.

My talents give me joy and freedom, heal me, and make me feel fulfilled. This situation concerns all women. Every time I hear about a woman leaving her real life for some 'prince', I am astonished again, though I know this type of men who demand their wives abandon everything they loves and likes as proof of love. I know them way too well.

The saddest aspect of this topic is that it is almost impossible for women like Grace not to become princesses locked in the golden cage. The pain of rejection they struggle with is unbearable, and even the biggest success won't help them. Unfortunately, marrying the prince doesn't help either, but this knowledge comes a little bit too late.

For people not equipped with the basic tools that make us independent and healthy, doing things well for them ('egoistic') is almost unreachable.

By 'basic tool,' I mean self-respect and a strong belief that we are worthy of love just as we are. We, people who were not loved in the crucial moment of life, when we were too small or too dependent on others to remember that, cannot choose the good for ourselves. Moreover, even if we try, we may experience unbearable pain. Yet, let us try.

I met a psychiatrist, who told me that she thinks that women in toxic relationships shouldn't leave their abusive partners, for it hurts them more than bruises and physical pain. This doctor was utter moron, not only in this case, because beaten woman may be simply killed by her "beloved" husband or boyfriend, just as alcohol or drugs kill addicted people and, not so rarely, people around them. However, I am convinced that leaving a lousy guy hurts as hell and, for the victim, it may look like the end of the world.

Still, doing one good thing just for me, like buying a flat, changes perspectives, sometimes drastically. Bad choices become harder to make, and there are more moments of hesitation.

But I won't beat about the bush - doing good things and making right choices doesn't heal, and the pain doesn't fade. On the contrary, the brain is like fire, for this is something unknown, odd, strange, and scary. Suddenly, the old demons are not only awakened, but they are furious since they are losing their prey. At this very moment, we need someone or something that will let us stay vertical, simply not to relapse or... commit suicide.

To illustrate this situation better, I need to use my example.

I made a choice. It was a perfect choice, but only while reasoning. Emotions were far from being rational... And the day of the ultimate test came. And it destroyed me. Since that day, I did lots of things - all to cope with this situation: writing new novel, going to the solicitor to terminate shitty agreement with my shitty publisher, launching on-line shop, going to Canary Islands... and many more.

That brain on fire... This ordeal... This must have happened because I cannot make right choices without feeling like a piece of crap.

It is very easy to judge people with mental issues and those who took their own lives as persons who are egoistic and focused only on themselves. Someone who doesn't know what these people are going through makes the assessments based on their own experience and superficial observations, not the complete picture of the situation.

I sometimes pass by one of the psychiatric hospitals while returning home after work. I see the patients sitting in the windows with metal bars, smoking, chatting, or just watching passersby like me. I know they are up there, not because of their egoism or laziness, and I know that people on the pavement around me tend to think that way.

"I have problems too - they think. - Yet I'm coping, trying, struggling... not pitying myself... I don't take a vacation from life."

On the other hand, the patients are somehow branded, sometimes mocked, as we hear the jokes about psychiatric wards and who should be there.

But there are two things I want to mention about being hospitalised. One is what the ward may do for us, and the second is what the ward doesn't do, but it should.

Luckily, these days, there are many decent hospitals and psychiatric wards, without bars mounted on windows and without cruel personnel. The patients wear regular clothes, spend time doing interesting things, and have unlimited access to beautiful parks or gardens. Those places create the opportunity to rest, both psychologically and physically, sometimes, for the first time in a very long time, e.g., for wives and mothers whose needs were neglected by the family. This is also the place where people who were abused, like me, after my service in the army, feel safe, protected by the chief of the ward from calls and unwanted visits. I know many stories of people, women mostly, who escape regularly to the hospital, and finally, as a result of sound therapy, they leave the toxic environment they lived in.

But the most important thing is that all the patients can be 'insane' legally and don't have to pretend anything anymore. In the ward, we all know that we suffer unbearable pain, and we learn how to treat ourselves well and with dignity. That's why it is so important to invest in psychiatric healthcare - this is society's input in helping many people do good things for themselves for the first time, and, as I wrote in previous posts, this one time may impact the whole life, not only of this one person...

Unfortunately, contemporary psychiatry, at least the one I came across, doesn't heal the main factor that makes us vulnerable and which pushes us into insanity. The doctors don't understand that, in many cases, they only deepen the 'black hole' in the patient's mind, unaware that the way to close it may be in their hands.

There is a tendency now to reverse the idea that all our problems in adult life come from relations with our parents. And I know why many shrinks withdraw from it - because they didn't see that this notion is helping the patients. But they're wrong. The thing is, people who had lousy parents still need a parent, even as grown-ups. They constantly ask questions, and the answers need to be given by a considerable authority, and there is no bigger one for the patient than the words of his or her psychiatrist. There are perfect conditions - the ward, the patient, the doctor's authority, the stage, the actors, roles to be played... However, the shrinks don't want to be compassionate or gentle; they don't want to react vividly and with indignation to the injustice that happened to the patient. Instead, they talk about forgiveness, forgetting, moving forward... They use medical terminology, make notes, and don't even look in the eyes. They lose the chance to save one life. They lose their patients, though, allegedly, it is the worst thing that may happen to the doctor.

Shitty Circumstances

For those who haven't experienced much love, it is usually a big problem to face: gaining other people's attention and 'buying' their 'love' that is so desperately needed, or not?

Behind this NOT, there is a whole spectrum of things to be done when we don't feel there is any need to look for fame and wealth, the 'love' can be bought with. And I know many people are unaware they have any other option: they don't have to be famous, rich, multitalented, or beautiful to be happy and satisfied. Because there is a straightforward logic of love we must understand: if we need to decline things that make us be loved, such 'love' we gain is not love whatsoever.

I repeat myself, but the topic is essential for me these days. I've learned the taste of being the real me, who is not fighting for anybody's admiration, who simply wants to do things that make me happy. Yet, the old matrix of emotions is still vivid in me; it constantly impacts my life. I am torn as if I were in two different worlds at the same time. But thanks to that, I can see very clearly how the world works and what really matters.

Just look at the entertainment. When someone has a talent, it is very easy to convince him or her that it is better to show the content that will be 'bought' by the masses, because, in most cases, being an artist of the heart doesn't sell well. Many people have been telling me that if I put sex into my novels, they will be more popular. Who knows, perhaps one day I will write a juicy erotic story, but only when I feel that I need it, not because this is a popular genre at the very moment.

So, I'm struggling every day. What to do? Which direction should I choose? It is so hard to be sure...

There is one way to acquire quite a high level of certainty in telling which way is right for me, since both forces are so strong. It is entrusted to God—total entrustment. And I am not writing about something very special, some prayers (which are almost impossible to say with the wounds made by my mother, nuns from my high school, and countless priests I encountered). It is about the circumstances we have no power to create. They are the most critical factors that help us change, forcing us to rethink everything and find people and the right words we should hear.

Of course, you may say that we are the ones who create the circumstances... And I will disagree. Many situations did or did not happen, and we don't even know about them. All these little tiny time shifts when we missed a train, read a book left by a stranger on the bench, or met some odd person... They plus our free will and a pinch of mind's effort may give extraordinary results, like repairing a broken soul or changing how our body reacts on certain occasions.

This way is the hardest, though the easiest one. Losing control is difficult, especially for someone who wants to control everything and everyone to create the circumstances to be with the loved one. Trusting the invisible Person is not a piece of cake either. And the moment you realise that the circumstances chosen by Heavens are hopeless (shitty?)... Yeah, this is a disaster. But what else can I do than accept it if I see I achieved so much through this strategy?

The Method of The Decade

Do you remember what you were doing ten, fifteen, or more years ago? I remember this day very well, precisely: 15 August 2008. I know what I had been doing, what I saw, what my thoughts were about, and what kind of mood I was in. Even though I had already made the decision to move to Warsaw, this exact day influenced me the most, at least for the first two years of living here.

Today, these things—so important back then—have faded or even disappeared. I do not regret making that decision, yet I am sure that now my motivations would be different. In fact, I am convinced that this is all about changing motivations, that I am making various choices because I am different, and that I came here to change myself. Simple as that.

I am not very glad about how my situation is developing, but I must be honest with myself and God (Whom I have some difficulties speaking with) that the direction is correct.

Seventeen years ago, I didn't know who I was whatsoever, and I wasn't always aware why I made these moves and not the others. And even when I gained that knowledge, I still had enormous difficulties choosing something else. But, as I wrote not once, it was all about making that first brave step and deciding differently, for my good. Yeah, buying a flat and taking a big mortgage for that was one of them, and it wasn't very wise as it was too big a challenge for me. Still...

I do not regret moving to the capital city, but there are many decisions I would have made a decade ago without any hesitation that are unacceptable to me now. What changed me that way? Painful experiences, good events, lots of thinking and praying, common sense, logic, and, of course, time to process all these elements. As a result, I've learnt how to choose the good even if it is not pleasant.

Philophobia

Do you know what is simple? The reason my mother didn't love me and was so mean to me. Because I loved and adored her. The more I loved, needed, and admired her, the more she hated and abused me. She was one of the many people who suffer from *philophobia*, the nasty condition when men and women are afraid of love. Nothing scares them more than the thought that someone loves them just as they are. Stupid shrinks say there is no rational explanation for this problem, that the mechanism is unknown... As I said, they are stupid because the reason is banal. Being loved and leading an everyday, happy life disrupts the constant telling of our true story by making wrong choices and hurting ourselves.

Unfortunately, this is like a snowball—bad events from childhood lead to bad choices in adult life, which lead to an even worse state. The wounds become bigger, the fear grows, and the phobia makes good relationships impossible.

Again, the only way to improve the situation is awareness. We must know what is really going on with us. I analysed my previous relationships and saw the pattern—people who know I love them hate me and hurt me. And I pretend they love me anyway. I see and hear things they didn't do or say. I don't bother with warning signals coming from them unless I avoid them from the very beginning.

With parents, the problem is even more complex, for almost everyone - family, church, friends, shrinks - convince us that mummy and daddy love us... Somehow, in the way they only know and understand, we must try to see facts that didn't occur. Hence, we ignore logic thinking and common sense, and, in the worst scenario, we cannot love and be with someone who loves us for real.

Honestly, men who truly loved me were ugly in my eyes, though they looked normal. I couldn't spend a minute in their presence. I was finding guys, sometimes bad looking, who could help me go through my 'story' once more: they saw their mothers they secretly hated in me, and I'd love them and be punished for that... Sick, right? Maybe yes, but not so uncommon.

B.S.

Unloved children often depend on their lousy parents so much that it sometimes costs them their lives (just remember the case of Peaches Geldof or Whitney Houston's daughter), and there is one particular reason for that: we constantly dwell on the 'whys'.

'Why was my mother so mean?'

'Why couldn't I do anything to change her?'

'Why did my father abandon me?'

'Why did my grandmother kill herself?'

And this is a huge mistake. Someone told us that if we understand, we will not judge. Well, at some point, this is BS, big and reeking BS. Even Jesus said that the sons shall be judges of their fathers *[Luke 11, 19]*. We must judge the deeds, not dwell on reasons, if we want the next generation to be better than this one.

I caught myself one day thinking, "Why? Why? Why? "What could I do or say to change the situation? "

I couldn't do a thing, for I wasn't in my parents' or grandparents' heads; they were completely different people, someone else... They did so much evil that the only thing I can do is not copy them, avoid them, cut myself off... and build the world based on God's law, not theirs.

The fourth commandment says we should honour our parents, but Jesus said: *"Anyone who does the will of God, that person is my brother and sister and mother."* [Mark 3,34] and, by this definition, my biological 'parents' were some strangers who hurt me and themselves.

The 'Westworld' TV series became more watchable for me when I realized that it is not about artificial intelligence per se, but is a gigantic allegory of human relations (just like 'Daybreakers', in fact, is not a movie about vampires).

Couple times at this blog, I was writing about staying in our own loops which we are not able to leave until we know the truth about us, until we are not the aware creatures instead of being puppets hanging on invisible strings steering by invisible, at the first glimpse, people - our Creators (parents in most cases). In the HBO show, the biggest loser among all intelligent machines is Theodore 'Teddy' Flood, because, as his creator said in one episode, he was equipped with only a 'vague feeling' that he had some sins on his conscience that made him unworthy of being happy. God, I felt such disdain towards this character that I almost missed that he was describing my own experience.

When I look back and I recall how I was feeling not so long ago, I could say the exact words as Teddy did: yeah, I dream about a better life, but I have some debts to pay and I cannot start a normal existence until I complete this task... Who wrote this scenario for me? Oh, I know the answer too well. But the most interesting thing is that my guilt and 'debit' on the conscience were only a 'vague belief', meaning, not so intensive and clear, yet very strong. Its strength was built on this blurry image, not a clear message.

I have been meeting such people throughout my life... People who didn't say anything clearly and coherently with their behaviour, thus I was feeling completely confused, just as I felt with my parents. They act like they can step back and say that nothing happened, for they didn't promise me a thing (even if they did promise), messed with others' heads, and preyed upon our weaknesses. These people should be despised and avoided because, in real life, they are ultimate losers. We need to remind ourselves of that fact more often.

Anhedonia

Something you may not know about people with 'suicidal brain' is that they are unable to experience pleasure in situations that, for most of the population, are pleasurable. So, it is complete nonsense to repeat relentlessly that 'you have no reason to feel badly, but there are many more to feel good and be grateful'. And I write these words from my experience - nothing that is happening with me and around me can improve my condition, nothing! The pain will come back anyway, the black hole in my soul will be even bigger, my wounds won't be healed...

I know it is challenging to understand, especially for the families of people who committed or tried to commit suicide. The kids or siblings of those persons dwell constantly on reasons and, not so often, are focused on everything good objectively. They think that, since parents or brothers or sisters had loving spouses, kids they were responsible for, they had a good, well-paid job, a beautiful house with a big garden, lots of friends, health, there was no sense in rejecting such a life... Yet, they couldn't stand another day in this paradise, for they didn't 'feel' it.

There is always the exhausting question of whether there was anything that could have helped and, at the same time, prevented this final act. Still, persistently repeating that there is no reason to be sad is not a good answer. So, don't say that to anyone, never! (Jesus, this is annoying even for sane people.)

I was wondering for months what I should have said to my late grandmother, and I found the answer when I realised that I am the one who needs to hear proper words. And these are like that:

"It will be tough for me if you do this, but I will respect any decision you make, for I respect you just as you are".

Thus, I understood what the fertiliser for our suicidal thoughts is: conviction that we are not free, that the only thing we may do independently, without being exposed to any judgement (even in our heads), is stepping aside, going away, terminating this whole ordeal once and forever. And, after all these affairs I have with my mother and her family, I am sure this might be the main problem in general, that somehow our lives seem to be prisons, cages with invisible bars. We cannot do things we want to do: tell loudly about our pain, because we are afraid that we will lose love and acceptance from other people.

Life is not pleasant for me, for it has been built on the wrong base: I need to deserve to be loved, e.g., by denying my true feelings, ergo my 'self.' The problem would disappear if I found someone, a colossal authority, who could understand my real situation, but no man could do that without accusing me of something and judging me at every step I made.

Euphoria

This symptom reveals itself in the most significant way in the case of people who have bipolar disorder (CHAD), but it concerns every unloved person I have been writing about for quite time. The feeling when the whole world is brightening, bursting with shining stars; suddenly, we are convinced that we can do whatever we want, that the pain from the phase of depression won't get back, like, never in our life... And, indeed, we do whatever we want, for we are smart and strong, very talented. After all, throughout our entire lives, we were learning various skills to gain people's attention and love. And now... Now, we conquer the world… until we fall.

The euphoria is our biggest enemy, for it sucks out our strength and vitality, but foremost it is a liar, imposter, a demon... It has two goals: to hide the truth about us and to destroy us from the inside. As a result, the inevitable phase of depression that follows is much worse than the one before.

Small euphoric states exist when we do or experience something that releases accumulated pressure. People become addicted to these 'small things', which turn into more significant issues. This is like pushing a specific button in our brains that stops feeling the pain for some time. But the source of this pain is still there, in our amygdala (or anywhere else, in the limbic system).

However, some people, like those who have bipolar disorder, prefer much bigger 'adventures', huge turnovers, significant changes, or challenges... And it wouldn't be anything wrong about it if it wasn't a regular addiction, but something that brings good and lasting results instead of destruction and relapse.

The worst thing about euphoria is the false conviction that the following change we are heading to may heal our wounds and free us from the shame and guilt we bear on our shoulders and in our hearts. This illusion may have fatal consequences, like marrying the wrong person, being a lousy parent, choosing the wrong professional path, and many others. The most common situation is when we think marriage is the way to repair everything that is wrong and painful. Society, families, and friends only confirm this conviction, even if their example shows something opposite.

I had a friend who so desperately wanted to find a husband that this pursuit influenced everything she did or talked about. I once asked her why she was so unrelenting and, in fact, unhappy because of that issue. She answered that her parents and grandma were constantly pushing her to do so. Her grandmother was especially fierce in this propaganda. So, I asked my friend whether this grandma was happy in her marriage.

"Oh, no! - the friend replied. - My grandpa was an awful husband for over fifty years."

"For God's sake! Then let her advise you in the area where she did succeed."

Of course, my friend didn't listen to me and was only euphoric for a short time. Her marriage turned out to be a total disaster, and the wound of being unloved became even bigger.

I discovered that the algorithm for making certain decisions is entirely different when I know my real condition, and the results won't heal me. My first thought was, "So nothing makes sense, there is no reason to wake up and try..."

Gritty Stamina

Someone put a link to the film on LinkedIn. A woman lectured about people who succeeded in something: graduating from a famous school, finishing a challenging project, building a big company, etc. The lecture was about why they succeeded and other people did not. I've learnt that this factor was always grit. Ok, that sounds right, but the speaker surprised me by saying that she doesn't know why some of us have it and that many of us are deprived of this essential virtue. And she and her co-workers don't know how to work it out with anybody.

Well, there are two things. One, why the hell would anyone work on anyone else's grit? Gosh! This smells like someone has an agenda here. Oh, I bet many parents want their kids to have the 'grit' to do things that are good for the parents, not for the kids. The same applies to employers who constantly ponder which part of the body and mind they should squeeze the employees so that they would be more efficient for them and, at the same time, satisfied with their useless and low-paid jobs.

I wouldn't dare install grit in anybody because it is closely related to a very individual matter: motivation. And this is thing number two.

This lady from the film must be utter moron since she doesn't know why some people can complete specific tasks even if they need to beat many obstacles while doing so. We won't do anything if we don't see or imagine the 'prize' at the end of our road. The more we want it, the stronger and more determined we are. The prize may be different for each of us, and we would be astonished to know what motivates others.

Sometimes, not so rarely, we don't succeed simply because we head for goals that are not for us. They don't fit our personality, character, abilities, talents... or just hearts. But sometimes, we don't succeed, yet just following that path makes us happy and satisfied. It all depends on what really motivates us.

I wrote that I lost my biggest motivation, which gave me strength and vitality... Yes, and the pain was unbearable, taking away my senses, devouring me from the inside. I thought that I was going to die, not literally, but that my soul would die, and I wouldn't do anything good in my life. It turned out that the old motivation was nothing, a joke, a pathetic joke... compared to how this pain motivates me and builds my grit.

No Success Is A Success

Many years ago, I was a nanny for a little boy with a sharp mind and always lots of things to say. I loved spending time with him, although his stupid parents said he was too sassy and annoying. I told him once to clean up his room, and of course, the boy didn't want to do so, but when he finally obeyed, he came to me and said: "Now, I want to be rewarded for what I've done. I am waiting for a compliment and some treat." Naturally, I explained to him that the world doesn't work like that, and we are not rewarded for things that are our duties. He didn't understand it then, but maybe now, when he's a student at the university, he knows it even without remembering that situation.

Or maybe not...

Lately, I realised that we tend to think like this boy, and it has become a very common tendency. We want to be rewarded for things we are obliged to do, and, what is even less logical, we sometimes name doing it a success.

Nowadays, people are addicted to this word. We constantly ponder what to do to be successful: whom to follow? Who is our guru? What actions should be undertaken? What should we think? What spell must we say?

Success depends on different factors: the country we come from, society, family, and our own empty skulls.

I am successful because of my big, smooth ass (I show without a shame on Instagram to hide my shallow personality).

I am successful because of my good job in a big corporation (although I am talented in different things).

I am successful because I drive an expensive car (which may be stolen at any minute and I don't even have proper insurance.

I am successful because I married a popular, rich, and famous guy (who, by the way, is an idiot).

Well, the success kills us. And it kills the most important thing for us: our duties.

When we ponder our fundamental duties, we lose sight of whether we are successful because our obligations are like something from another universe.

Success ensures euphoria—well, at least for one short moment—which is why it is addictive and not satisfying or healing.

People who crave success so badly that they sometimes do stupid things are unloved children. I know that because I didn't experience love from my parents, and I tasted this hunger for success in anything that would prove I am worthy of love.

Now, look around. You will see many unloved people who crave attention (likes and followers on social media) and acceptance. You may think that we are surrounded only by sick persons deprived of love because we can see and hear them everywhere. Yes, the lack of love may be very garish and loud.

The truth is, people who know they are loved very often are invisible because they are busy doing the necessary things. They fulfil their duties and don't even think someone can praise them for that.

The best examples are mothers and fathers. It is almost certain that parents who demand gratitude and compliments for their work are bad parents. They are focused on themselves and on how they are seen by society, not on the needs of their children.

I am firmly convinced that we all are parents, even without our own offspring. We meet kids and teenagers every day, and what we say or do is as important as the words and deeds of their parents. We may sometimes save somebody's life with a simple gesture they didn't experience at home. And this is not something extra for which we should be rewarded—this is our duty.

The first and most important thing we must do is tell the truth. We must discover it, learn how this world should function, who we really are, what is good for us and others, and how to live. The second thing, coming directly from the previous one, is developing our talents. I am a writer and good at that, so there is nothing extraordinary in writing and publishing novels. I will be judged for that.

But what to do if we are not loved and we suffer so much that success seems to be the only thing that can help us in our misery? I am aware that the euphoria will vanish, and I will suffer even more. So, how can we get out of this impasse?

I can see only one solution: behave like you are loved, even if you don't feel it.

The true Reason

Since I was a tiny girl, I knew my mother wanted to hurt me. It was a firm conviction, yet so scary that I had to suppress it by any means to survive. I had to 'conjure' her love in my head, literally produce it, otherwise my body would not live.
However, there was a catch – my catch-22, which I hadn't recognized for a long time. To gain her 'love,' I not only had to betray who I was, but I had to kill myself.
And it's not a figure of speech.

After her death, I had to clean up her stuff, which included an enormous pile of papers, some dated as far back as 1960. And there I found the ultimate proof that I was not wrong in believing she wanted to murder me.
She kept the receipt from the hospital for the abortion. My abortion.
She wanted to fulfil her dreams and go abroad to Syria as a military nurse. I knew this part of the story, but I wasn't aware that she did everything she could to make her dreams come true. She was 22nd week pregnant; however, she told the doctors it was 18th week... I knew it was a lie, as my biological father disclosed the precise date of my conception. Moreover, she admitted many times that she went into labor at 42nd weeks of pregnancy, and on the receipt for my birth, it was 38th weeks. At least she was consistent with her lies.
So, she had spent eleven days in the gynaecology ward attempting to get rid of me. I was big, too big for a 'standard' procedure of removing my body from her uterus (today, I would be torn apart by a gruesome surgery), so they used many chemical agents to kill me and to make her womb unable to carry a child. They failed.
If you met my non-mother, you'd learn she wasn't giving up easily when pursuing her dreams. During the labor, she

refused to cooperate and pushed me out. She wanted to suffocate me, and it wasn't the last time she tried this trick. The personnel stepped into action and did their job by using techniques applied during the birth of stillborn babies. Literally, someone else gave birth to me because my mother was too busy with her business. Of course, doctors and nurses became very vigilant and noticed on time when she tried to starve me to death, while we were still on the ward. It was close! I know that from my friend's mother, who fed me with her milk and saved my life.

I am all shaken when I think of how many times she attempted to hurt me. Yet, it's good to be together with these feelings and connect them with actual events that didn't come easily.
Six months after her death, I had a major emotional breakdown. One night, I started looking for the highest possible and accessible building in my neighbourhood to jump from it and end my life. Instead, I caught the tram and went to the psychiatrist. Naturally, they helped me, just as my friends who organized a nice vacation for me. I only had this one nagging thought: why jump?
And then I had an epiphany.

When I was four, she showed me the window and suggested it…
It was a whopping four-floor distance straight into a concrete staircase leading to the basement.
My body learned that day that my mother wants me to end my life since she failed. However, my mind didn't accept it.

My suicide would mean one thing: this bitch won.

And I won't give her this satisfaction.

www.ingramcontent.com/pod-product-compliance
Lightning Source LLC
Chambersburg PA
CBHW032121280326
41933CB00009B/935